THE TATZELWURM

THE ORIGINAL DRAGON ?

by

James Foster Robinson

CONTENTS

INTRODUCTION

The scale covered creature swoop down on huge wings and breathed fire upon its victims. In Europe in bygone ages, this creature, the dragon, terrorized the countryside until a hero rode forth and slayed this evil. In this book we will look at the creature that may have been the basis of the dragon stories and it just may have survived in the European Alps until quite recently. It is the Tatzelwurm!

THE LEGEND

A depiction of Saint George slaying the dragon shows a creature with a snake-like body, two front legs with claws and possibly a cat face. Did Saint George fight and slay a Tazelwurm? What is a Tazelworm? It is a creature said to have lived and may still live in the mountains of Europe, especially Austria, Switzerland and the Principality of Liechtenstein. This creature could well have been the prototype for the dragons of legend. In this book we will take a look at the supposedly mythical creature and consider if there is evidence that encounters with the Tatzelwurm and its kin may have inspired the legends of dragons, at least in Europe and maybe the world.

THE ANIMAL

NAMES

Tatzelwurm is German for "clawed worm." Its scientific name, given by Jakob Nicolussi in 1933, is Heloderma europaeum.

The Tatzelwurm is known by a number of names according to the region it was found in. In parts of Switzerland, it was called the Stollenwurm (Tunnel or hole dwelling worm) and Stollwurm ("hole worm") in the Bernese Alps of Switzerland,. In the Swiss Alps, the Tatzelwurm is also known by many as the 'Alps Dragon'. It was called the Bergstutzen (mountain stump), and the Springwurm, which stood for "jumping worm") in Tirol, Austria. It was known as the Lindwurm in Innsbruck, Austria. Basilisco (basilisk) or the milk-serpent was its name in Northern Italy. Local Italian legend purports that it sucks milk from cows' utters on the pastures. Other names include Springwurm (Jumping Worm), Daazelwurm, Praatzelwurm and Arassas (French Alps). DARD, Höckwurm and Kuschka (from the Slovenian kuscar, "lizard") were some other names from various regions in Europe. In some regions, the

Tatzelwurm is also called the Cat-snake or Cat-Headed Snake because of its cat-like head. The name Tatzelwurm itself means clawed serpent or worm.

DESCRIPTION

Anonymous Artist's Illustration of the Tatzelwurm via Wikimedia Commons

From these names we get a simple description of the creature. It looked like stumped or short worm like serpent of unknown weight, had either a cat-like or dragon-like face, bright glowing eyes, lived in the mountains, could jump, and had claws. The literature and reports about it reveals more. The creature was between two and six feet long, some times with only two legs in the front part of it body and sometimes four. Regardless of the number of legs, it had three toes with very sharp claws on each leg. Its blood was supposedly like acid and it had a poisonous breath lethal enough to kill humans.

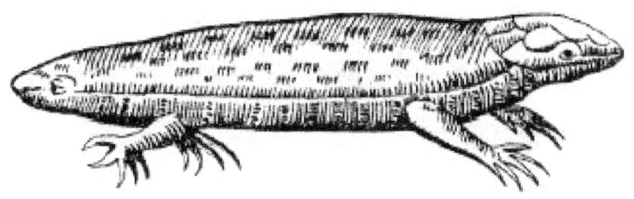

It is interesting to note that nearly all drawings of the Tatzelwurm show what looks like a pinecone or cigar on four stubby legs and with tiny eyes instead of the feline face mention in a large number of eye witness reports.

One writer felt that this discrepancy did not mean anything as drawings of known animals years ago often looked only slightly like the real animal observed. The drawings of the Tatzelwurm are consistent in themselves and the encounter reports are consistent in themselves but are not consistent all together. Did the first artist not believe that witnesses were accurately describing what they saw and drew what he thought they saw and other artists followed suit? Whatever was the case, it is unlikely that issue will even be resolved unless a specimen of a real Tatzelwurm is found and properly identified.

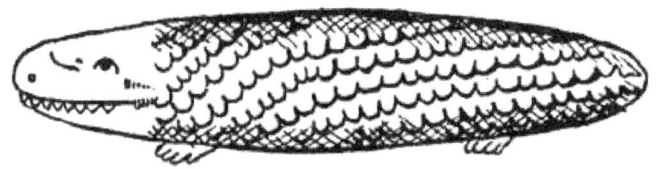

Most eye witness accounts seem to agree that the Tatzelwurm looked like a lizard or snake with smooth hairless skin covered with delicate scales and grew up to at least six feet in length. The creature had two small legs in front but seemed to be missing hind legs or had vestigial appendages. Its head resembled a cat with big eyes but had scales instead of fur.

The Tatzelwurm is known to be extremely ferocious and will not run away from humans. It fact, it will attack and try to bite the person while emitting a high pitch sound.

The Tazelwurm in Swiss folklore was a dragon-like creature with four legs, claws and breathed poison or fire. In some accounts, it had a lizard's head or a cat's face as well as a very long tail, bristles and scales. A blade or stick was said to not be able to pierce these scales as they were very thick. The creature was able to stand on its hind legs. Its diet consisted of lost children and unattended cattle. The animal's home was often in mountain caves

Several illustrations of the Tatzelwurm exist. The Bavarian hunting manual called New Pocket Guild of the Year 1836 for Nature, Forest and Hunting Enthusiasts contained what Bernard Heuvelmans, a Naturalist or scientist, said was a curious picture of a scaly, cigar-shaped creature with sharp teeth and feet like little stumps. Another illustration in the Swiss almanac Alpenrosen from 1841contained a drawing of a long, scaly creature with two very small front legs.

A Mr. Balkin, a Swiss photographer, claimed to have taken a picture of a Tatzelwurm. The publication of this photograph generated such interest that the Berliner Illustrierte, a weekly illustrated magazine in Germany, sponsored an expedition to hunt for a living example of the creature. The expedition conducted in winter was unsuccessful. This might have been possible due to the possibility that the Tatzelwurm, not being a warm blooded animal, was hibernating. Interest in the creature quickly waned. Many of today's cryptozoologists believe that Balkin's photograph was a hoax.

HABITAT
The Tazelwurm was usually found in mountainous

terrain like the Alps. It lived in burrows or holes or tunnels. It is also thought to also be aquatic in that some sighting placed it in or near water.

RANGE

The Tazelwurm range included the Alps in Europe mainly in the countries of Switzerland, Liechtenstein, Austria, France and Italy, and the surrounding lower lands.

SIGHTINGS

In the summer of 1717, Joseph Scherer, a herb and root collector from 'Näfels', was digging some roots at the foot of the 'Glärnisch Hirschenzungen' (mountain). His son was picking flowers when the boy shrieked loudly. Joseph rushed over and found his son staring in fright at what appeared to be a rock from under which a gruesome animal hissed. It had a cat-like head with two wild, protruding, sparkling eyes. When he tried to scare the strange creature away, it came out of its hole. This cat-beast had four short legs ending in claws on its spotted, scale covered body. Whipping its long tail from side to side, it looked like it was ready to jump at the man and his son. Scherer quickly sharpened a stick and pierced the animal with it. The stick easily penetrated the animal's flesh. Poisonous and stinking blood splashed out of its wound and a few drops landed on the man's leg. His leg immediately swell up greatly and Scherer had to limp home in great pain. It took a month of doctoring and putting salve on it before the swelling went down. All his neighbors were sure that he had killed a "dragon". The local name for that creature and its kin was 'Lindwurm'?

In 1779, a man named Hans Fuchs encountered two Tazelwurms in his pig pen. He was so frightened that he suffered a heart attack while running back to his house. He was able to tell his family about the encounter before he died. Hans described one creature as having a snake like body five to seven feet in length, a large feline-like head with sharp teeth and clawed front legs. A relative painted a picture of Hans meeting the Tazelwurms. It shows two big lizard-like creatures in the background. The German cryptozoologist, Ulrich Magin, apparently felt that this painting was the best evidence of the Tazelwurm's existence. What do you think?

There is a story that some experts believe is unlikely. In 1828, a peasant in the Solothrun Canton found a corpse of a Tazelwurm in a dried out marsh. He set it aside apparently intending to take it home after he finished his work. Alas, apparently some hungry crows had eaten the corpse leaving only the skeleton. The man took the bones to the town of Solothurn. The authorities decided to sent it to Heidelburg where it simply disappeared. Thus the "unlikely" tag on the story.

That did not stop people from believing that the Tazelwurm was real. Perhaps a number of mountain dwellers had encounters of their own and, for some reason, told no one or just their family and friends. The creature may have even been rare back in the 1800's. It was thought to be extinct but sightings have been reported in recent years. But some of these sightings may be of another entirely different creature.

In 1861, the Swiss naturalist Friedrich von Tschundi, convinced that the creature was real, wrote that the belief in Tatzelwurms was wide spread in Bernese Oberland and the Jura. This creature was a thick "cave worm" with two short legs and was 30 to 90 cm long. It was often seen when storms approached after a long dry spell.

In July 1883 or 1884, Kaspar Arnold was at a mountain restaurant on the Spielberg, near Hochfilzen, Tirol, Austria when he spied and watched for twenty minutes a strange creature with only two legs. He was sure that it was the elusive Tatzelwurm.

Around 1917, a young farm girl from an 'Oberhof' or upper farm in Switzerland was cutting bean poles from trees in the mountain forest of 'Saal' when she encounter a Tatzelwurm. She was working hard on a young fir stem that had three evenly protruding roots forming a hollow space under it when a young 'Stollenwurm' (Tunnel worm - another name for Tatzelwurm) rushed out of the hole and attacked the girl. The creature was about two feet long, grey in color with its midbody as thick as a cat. Its head had two ears that were fleshy, hairless, round cut and upright. On its face were two large, bright, round eyes. The creature walked on two short front legs that had small wide paws. It should also be noted that it was a hot summer when this event occurred.

In the summer of 1921, two people were surprised by a two legged Tatzelwurm when it leaped nine feet in the air toward them near Rauris, Salzburg, Austria. They describe the creature as being grey in color with a head like a cat and was two to three feet long.

In 1924, two men claimed to have found a five-foot -long skeleton which allegedly resembled a lizard at an unspecified location.

In 1929, an Austrian school teacher, while rummaging around in a cave on the Tempelmauer, encountered what seemed to be a giant salamander. He described it as a snake-like animal with smooth, almost white scale-less skin, flat head and two very short feet at the forefront of its body. The feet were short and atrophied but had no claws. This creature was estimated to be no more than forty or forty-five centimeters long. The teacher felt that this "Tatzelwurm" was a rare species of salamander that lived in moist caves rarely seeing the light of day.

Two investigators, Dr Gerhard Venzmer and Hans Fulcher, recorded sixty eyewitnesses reports in the

1930s all of which described a thirty to sixty centimeter (one to two feet) long creature with a scaly, cylindrical body, an abrupt ending tail, no neck, large eyes and it hissed like a snake. Does some it sound familiar? In addition, similar reports came in from France, Italy and Sicily.

In 1954, as mentioned above, the Swiss photographer, Balkin supposedly photographed a Tatzelwurm that he found resting by a log near Meiringen, Switzerland. He was taking a picture of an unusual log. When the bulb flashed, the "log" ran away. It is now believed that his photo was probably a faked image of a ceramic fish.

In the 1960's, a Geneva, Switzerland, newspaper received a photograph supposedly of a Tatzelwurm from unknown persons. Many cryptozoologists and researchers who examined the picture believe it is a hoax.

A resident of Lengstein, Trentino-Alto Adige, Italy reported seen in the summer of 1969 a thirty inch long animal that had two hind legs and seemed to be able to inflate its neck. This does not sound like a Tatzelwurm and maybe was a lizard someone released or it escaped. I thought I would throw it into the mix. Later in October 1991 and September 1992, a gray, crested reptile, zigzagging or darting around on Pizzo Cronia in the same area was reported by a Giuseppe Costale.

A number of reports about sightings of the Tatzelwurm appeared in the Swiss newspaper, La Tribune de Geneve, by Georges Hardy in the 1970's. I have not been able to find any more information about them.

A creature that looked like a Tatzelwurm was spotted in Denmark in June of 1973. This is a little far afield from its usual haunts and may have been an escaped or released pet lizard.

In 1990, the skeleton of a lizard-like animal was found by two naturalists in the Alps near Domodossola, Italy. Nothing is known at the time of writing if the skeleton was identified or were it is now.

Then in April 2007, a young boy in Upper Austria claimed to have seen a brown lizard, fifty centimeters long, on the Enns River bank near Ternberg. Tatzelwurm sightings were quite common, they say, in that area in the 19th Century. The creature that the boy saw was reported to be just an escaped exotic pet lizard. Maybe it was and maybe it wasn't. Partly eaten snakes had been found along the river. Searches of the river and its banks however found nothing.

In the several years before 2009, the residents of the community of Tresivio in the Valtelina Valley, a part of Italy bordering on Switzerland, saw a weird creature which they described as an "agile bipedal lizard, about a metre tall and nearly two metres long." This sounds very much like a living dinosaur and not a Tatzelwurm, but it will do in a pinch. It was first seen by an agricultural sciences student. She said it resembled a prehistoric veloci-raptor and was somewhat like a monitor lizard. However this creature walked on two hind legs while its anterior legs were very small. Monitors walk on all four legs and not just the hind legs. She also said that it was one and a half to two meters long with its head a meter and its back eighty centimeters above the ground.

Then, in July of 2007, the creature was seen again by residents of the villages of Tresivio and Ponte. The witnesses were adamant that it was not an Iguana and was running. Also, in July, a similar creature, if not the same one, was seen by a farmer from Ponte when he parked his tractor on a road to the Val Fontana above the village. The creature resembled a kangaroo but was a lizard with scales and a long tail.

On 28 September 2009, at about 2:30 pm, Giovanni Pianezzola, a resident of Vallonara spotted a strange reptile in his garden. He described it as being brown in color and a meter long. The creature apparently ran out of the garden and disappeared into the Longhella River. At first he thought it may have been an escaped alligator but his neighbors felt that it was just a harmless Basilisco or cat-serpent which was well known in the area. Hmmm! Cat-serpent - maybe a Tazelwurm?

An anonymous witness reported that on two occasions, October 4th and 5th of 2009, he encountered a very strange reptile on the banks of the Longhella River between Marostica and Vallonara in Venetia, a north-eastern province of Italy between Lake Garda and Venice. He thought that this creature might have been a caiman, iguana or monitor lizard, none of which are native to the region. The man said that it was at least a meter long. A search by police found nothing resembling a giant reptile. It should be noted here that the locals reported that ducks were disappearing from the river. At first, a giant carp was blamed but now people had a different culprit in mind.

LEGEND OR REALITY?

Sometime in the 1900's, a skeleton thought to be that of a Tatzelwurm was donated to the Geneva Institute of Science under mysterious circumstance. The only evidence of it remaining is a single photograph showing a long snake like creature with two clawed arms and a larger than normal head. It is now believed that the supposed skeleton and the photo are part of a hoax.

For now, there is no concrete physical evidence of the existence of the Tatzelwurm. However, as more research is devoted to the subject, good evidence may yet be uncovered.

I do, however feel, that the Tatzelwurm is a real creature, rare now, but quite common in the Aps years ago. There are too many eyewitness reports to say otherwise.

WHAT IS THE TATZELWURM?

Many interested people have suggested all sorts of explanations as to what the Tatzelwurm might be. I have included a number of them in this section .

GILA MONSTER?

Released into the public domain by its author, Arpingstone as per http://commons.wikimedia.org/wiki/File:Gila.monster.arp.jpg

The man considered by most to be the father of Crytozoology, Bernard Heuvelmans, felt that the Tatzelwurm may be related to America's Gila monster that lives in that country's southwest. The similarities in habitat such as living in a burrow, the use of poison or venom against it's prey and enemies does make a case but the Tatzelwurm's reports as having bright eyes and cat-like face can be used to argue otherwise. Apparently, no known salamander, which a Gila Monster is, has those two telling characteristics. Unless of course, the many eyewitnesses were wrong.

GIANT SALAMANDER?

Japanese Giant Salamander public domain as per were http://en.
wikipedia.org/wiki/File:Cryptobranchus_japonicus.jpg

A species of giant salamander is said to have existed in the European Alps a long time ago. And some species of salamanders have legs that have shriveled up over time. This might account from the description of the Tatzelwurm having only two legs in front. Also with hind legs almost none existent, the creature might have been more at home in water even though it could get around with its front legs. Hiding in burrows and in water, would explain the rare sightings of the animal. The Chinese giant salamander (Andrias davidianus), can grow to more than six feet in length. If the Tatzelwurm is or was related to it, as suggested by Ulrich Magin, then it could have easily been the model for the stories of dragons.

OTTER

Some investigators believe that this mysterious creature might just simply be an unknown species of otter. However, the eyewitness descriptions do not support this theory as the Tatzelwurm described does not have fur and does not even remotely resemble the Otter.

GIANT LIZARD

La Gomera giant lizard. In public domain as per http://en. wikipedia.org/wiki/File:Gallotia_bravoana.jpg

The Tatzelwurm as a Giant Lizard as opposed to a giant salamander would explain its preying on animals on land. But a lizard with poorly developed or nonexistent back legs does not fit the parameters of the description of a Tatzelwurm.

SNAKE

Now snakes are a possibility except for the lack of legs. Some have speculated that the Tatzelwurm with its good front legs and diminutive or nonexistent back legs might be an evolutionary connection between snakes and lizards. But once again, snakes fail to meet all the requirements in eyewitness descriptions.

LAKE MONSTER/SEA SERPENT

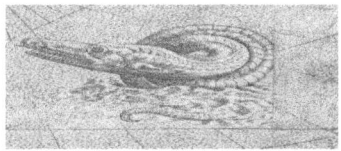

One or more persons have tried to explain the

Tatzelwurm as a sea or lake monster. It is thought that they travel briefly overland from one small alpine lake to another.

MEXICAN MOLE LIZARD

Licensed under the Creative Commons Attribution 2.0 Generic as per http://en.wikipedia.org/wiki/File:Bipes_biporus.jpg

The Mexican Mole Lizard is a possible candidate as the Tatzelwurm does somewhat resemble it. Unfortunately, the Mexican Mole Lizard is very small and is usually only found in Mexico. It is highly unlikely that even a distance relative of the Mexican Mole Lizard could have survived in the mountains.

LUNGFISH

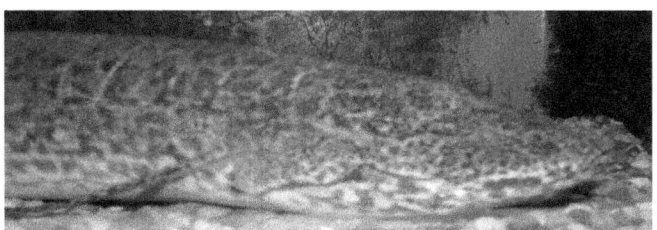

A Zoologist, Richard Freeman, felt that the Tatzelwurm might be similar or related to the Australian Lungfish (Neoceratodus forsterihas) a member of a bizarre group of fish. Nature has modified their air bladders so that they can gulp air as if they had lungs. This ability allows them to survive in a drought. I fail to see the connection.

TALL TALES, HALLUCINATIONS OR MISTAKEN IDENTITY

Another possibility is that sightings of the Tatzelwurm are simply the result of tall tales, hallucinations or mistaken identity. To accept this hypothesis, you would have to disregard the many similar details in witnesses testimonies over the years and from many different locations. But some but not all may be just that. That still leaves a lot of valid sightings.

THE ORIGINAL DRAGON?

Are the encounters with the Tatzelwurm the basis for the legends of Dragon? The Tatzelwurm appears to have been native to the mountainous regions of Europe. The European Dragon is also native to the same area. The tales told of both are very similar. Both lived in holes in the ground or caves. Both had scaly hides. Some of the earlier descriptions reported that the dragon had a cat like face, two front legs and a tail just like the Tatzelwurm. The dragon swopped down on its victims and burned them with its fiery breath. The Tatzelwurm was known to leap from high rocks or from the ground at its victims. The bite of the Tatzelwurm was said to be poisonous and burned those so bit. The dragon in flight may have been added in the later tales. Stories do grow with the telling.

The German term "Wurm" means "worm" in English and was used to describe a snake like creature that lived in the ground.

Many locals in the Alps use the terms "Wurm" and "dragon" to describe the same creature that they are used to seeing in their region.

The creature was so accepted in the Alps that it appeared in several books on Alpine natural history and hunting along with more familiar animals.

Now, I know that the above is not definite proof that the Tatzelwurm was the original dragon. But is is a good start for someone who wanted to investigate further. I am not a scientists or an academic but I do see a possible connection between the two creatures. W hat do you think?

As a storyteller of some small skill, I am well aware how a story can grow in the telling and become something more then it was originally. I am reminded of a story about a haunted table I made up many years ago over a jug of draught in Finnigan's at the Frontenac Hotel in Kingston, Ontario. Six month later, the same story, embellished and reportedly on good authority that it was true - the girl who told me said that she knew the man who knew the man it happened to - was told to me. I, of course, pretended that I never heard it before.

The point is that stories can have a true beginning and change with each telling. Below is an example of what I feel might have happen to the Tatzelwurm on its journey to dragonhood.

Johann' Story

I was walking along a trail high up in the Alps on my way to a friend's farm. When I approached a large boulder, a strange creature leaped off the top of it and attacked me. Where it bit me on my upraised arm, I felt a burning sensation and smelt a terrible odor. Knocking it to the ground, I ran quickly down the path to home. There, my family treated my wound which looked like a burn while I told my story. I described this terrible creature as about six feet long, two small legs with claws at the front and a long tail. Its head was like that of a cat and it had large shinning eyes that glared at me with a terrifying look. It skin was smooth but was covered with what looked like scales. This creature is common here about's and is called a Tatzelwurm.

A Fiend of Johann's Version Told Later To Others

My friend Johann was attacked by a ferocious creature in the mountains the other day. It flew off a large rock and wounded him with a terrible bite that burned him bad. The wurm was long with two front legs, a ferocious cat-like face as well as a scaly body. Johann was lucky to escape with his life.

A Friend of A Friend of Johann's Version Some Time Later.

A friend of my friend was attacked and burned by a ferocious creature that dropped down out of the sky one day up in the mountains. The creature had big terrifying eyes that paralyzed the poor man. Luckily, he was able to get safely away with only some bad burns. Beware that these wurms or dragons live high up in the mountains and will attack people.

A Down The Road Version
Beware of the mountains as there are flying dragons that swoop down out of the sky and attack unwary strangers burning them to death. One man told how his daughter went up those mountains alone one day and never returned. We could not search for her as there was a terrible lighting storm up there. The next day, we found her body covered in burns beside that of a burnt tree. The dragon must have swopped down out of the sky and killed her with its fiery breath. Tell your young maidens not to go up in those mountains as dragons will kill them with their fiery breath and eat them.

There you have it - my admittedly simple version of how a story or experience can get retold and retold until it is no longer like the original one. I feel that in this way sightings of the real Tatzelwurm became tales of the mythical dragon.

Here is an party game you an play with children of all ages. It works really well with children (Adults) who have had a bit to drink. Have them line up and then whisper a sentence or two into the ear of the first person. Then each person in turn whispers it to the next person. The last person in the line then tells what he or she heard out loud. Do not be surprised if it is very different from what you whispered in that first ear. That is how, I believe, the Tatzelwurm became the Dragon and the Tatzelwurm/Dragon may still be up there in the Alps just waiting to make our acquaintance.

]

REFERENCES
INTERNET

bp.blogspot.com/-F3X_3xVjPPE/TrG-2j1UEfI/AAAAAAAAaOQ/z_zTyFbmNA4/s1600/tatzel4.jpg

bp.blogspot.com/-WVm0TNePaSQ/TrG-Gju5P3I/AAAAAAAAaNs/1KRA7Bf4c7M/s1600/tatzel2.JPG

bp.blogspot.com/-8y-OMPln82E/TrG-U8PcpKI/AAAAAAAAaN4/rjrR8yRTm-M/s1600/tatzel1.jpg

bp.blogspot.com/-7RxRjCQwj-c/TrG-k425OTI/AAAAAAAAaOE/DUPbscF0sUY/s1600/tatzel3.jpg

cryptozoologycryptids.wikia

carnivoraforum.com/topic/9702723/1/images4.wikia

cryptozoologycryptids.wikia.com/wiki/FileTatzelwurm.jpg

cryptozoologycryptids.wikia.com/wiki/FileTatzelwurm_Pic..jpg

cryptozoologycryptids.wikia.com/wiki/UserAzelf5000

cryptozoologycryptids.wikia

com/wiki/Tatzelwurmimages3.wikia.en.wikipedia.org/wiki/Tatzelwurm

cryptozoologycryptids.wikia.com/wiki/Tatzelwurm

forteantimes.com

itsnature.org

levelbeyond.com

naturalplane.blogspot.com/2011/11/tatzelwurm-alps-dragon.html

newanimal.org

nocookie.net/__cb20110719202251/cryptozoologycryptids/images/5/56/Tatzelwurm.jpg

nocookie.net/__cb20110719202857/cryptozoologycryptids/images/f/ff/Tatzelwurm_Pic..jpg

unknownexplorers.com

wiki.ffxiclopedia.org/wiki/Stollenwurm

wiki.ffxiclopedia.org/wiki/Tatzlwurm

wiki.ffxiclopedia.org/wiki/Tunnel_Worm

wormwoodchronicles.com

www.amazon.com/exec/obidos/ASIN/0393322114/shapeshiftere-20

www.amazon.
com/exec/obidos/ASIN/0684856026/shapeshiftere-20

www.amazon.
com/exec/obidos/ASIN/0786420367/shapeshiftere-20

www.amazon.
com/exec/obidos/ASIN/1578590701/shapeshiftere-20

www.forteantimes.
com/features/articles/5179/the_tatzelwurm_lives.html

www.itsnature.org/legendary-creatures/tatzelwurm/

www.monstropedia.org/index.php?
title=Tatzelwurm#ixzz2GNajuDZX www.monstropedia.
org/index.php?title=Tatzelwurm

www.monstropedia.org/index.php?
title=Tatzelwurm#ixzz2GNassXri www.monstropedia.
org/index.php?title=Tatzelwurm

www.monstropedia.org/index.php?
title=SpecialBookSources/1931044643

www.monstropedia.org/index.php?
title=Tatzelwurm#ixzz2GNawtOgG www.monstropedia.
org/index.php?title=Tatzelwurm

www.newanimal.org/buru.htm

www.newanimal.org/c-dragons.htm. ....

www.newanimal.org/salaman.htm

www.newanimal.org/tatzel.htm

www.unknownexplorers.
com/cryptogallery/hybrids/hybridsgallery/tatzelwurm/galler
y.html

www.unknownexplorers.com/tatzelwurm.php

Books, Magazines

Fortean Times *FT272,* FT20846-49

Clark, Jerome and Coleman, Loren. Cryptozoology A-Z New York Simon & Schuster, 1999. Pages 231 -232

Clark, Jerome. Unexplained! Detroit Visible Ink Press, 1999. Pages 283, 363-365

Freuler, Kaspar, and Thürer, Hans, Glarner tales, 1968.

Frick, Tales from the Fricktal", 1987/88

Giornale di Vicenza, 6 Oct 2009.

Giornale di Vicenza, 7 Oct 2009.

Il Giorno, 7 Aug 2009

Newton, Michael. Encyclopedia of Cryptozoology
A Global Guide to Hidden Animals and Their
Pursuers Jefferson, North Carolina McFarland &
Company, 2005. Pages 90, 452

ORF, 3 May; Oberösterreichische Nachrichten, 3
May; 4 May; Standard, 8 May 2007.

Rose, Carol. Giants, Monsters and Dragons,
Denver ABC-CLIO, 2000. Pages 346, 355

Shuker, Karl. The Beasts That Hide From Man
Seeking the World's Last Undiscovered Animals
New York Paraview Press, 2003. Pages 177-182

About the Author

James Foster Robinson was born in Ogdensburg, New York, USA but grew up in Prescott, Ontario, Canada. He has lived and worked in Ontario, Manitoba, Alberta and British Columbia. In 2005, he moved to West Virginia and married his present wife, Betty. Jim has two books published by Mika Publishing, Belleville, Ontario Amazing Tales from Eastern Ontario, 1987; Strange But True Tales From Eastern Ontario, 1989. He has also published numerous articles in national magazines, daily and weekly newspapers. While living in Vancouver, BC, Jim was a Feature Writer on Suite101.com for topics - The Art of Storytelling, Storyteller's Korner, Sleep Disorders, Professional Security, and Liechtenstein. In addition, he was a Storyteller both in Kingston, Ontario and in Vancouver, BC, Canada. James has also published "A Ghostly Guide to West Virginia", "An Encyclopedia of Lake and River Monsters", "Riotous Times, An Unauthorized History of Riots and Violent Protests in British Columbia, Canada", "British Columbia Weird", "A Ghostly Guide to Kentucky", "A Ghostly Guide To California", "A Ghostly Guide to Tennesse", "West Virginia Weird and Wonderful", "Ghost Lights, Spook Lights, Will o' Wisps and Friends", a novel "Umpock - The Hole In The Ground" and a children book "Tales To Tell My Children" on Amazon.com. He is presently working on Ghostly Guides to the remaining 46 states as well as several novels.